animal hospital

Official annual 2001

Written by Jane Clempner

Photography by Steve Gorton and Barry Boxall

Front cover photograph by Karen Wright

Designed by Traffika Publishing Limited

Illustrated by Terry Riley, Liz Sawyer, Helen Prole Peter Wilks, and Debbie Clarke

With thanks to the staff at the RSPCA Putney Animal Hospital, the RSPCA Harmsworth Animal Hospital and the RSPCA Manchester Animal Hospital, for making time in their busy schedules to help with this book.

Photographs:
Page 12: *Golden Retriever* RSPCA Photolibrary ' Andrew Forsyth
Page 16: *Young Gull* RSPCA Photolibrary ' Kate Huntly; *Fox Cub in Woodland in Springtime* RSPCA Photolibrary ' Angela Hampton; *Ginger and White Cat Sitting in the Sun* RSPCA Photolibrary ' Julie Meech; *Mistle Thrush* RSPCA Photolibrary ' Ross Hoddinott; *Dutch Guinea Pig* RSPCA Photolibrary ' E A Janes; *Goldfish* RSPCA Photolibrary ' Joe B Blossom
Page 17: *Hedgehog in Autumn Leaves* RSPCA Photolibrary ' Stuart Harrop; *Greenfinch Male on Wire Peanut Feeder* & *Mallard* RSPCA Photolibrary ' Mark Hamblin; *Albino Guinea Pig* RSPCA Photolibrary ' Andrew Forsyth
Page 28: *Ginger and White Hamster* RSPCA Photolibrary ' Angela Hampton
Pages 44, 45, 46 & 47 Stapeley Grange Wildlife Hospital photographs RSPCA Photolibrary ' Robin Culley
Page 58: *Mexican Red-Kneed Tarantula* RSPCA Photolibrary ' E A Janes

Animal Hospital wordmark and logo are trademarks of the British Broadcasting Corporation and are used under licence. Animal Hospital logo ' 1998. Licensed by BBC Worldwide Ltd.
Photographic images supplied to the Licensee by BBC Worldwide Ltd ' 2000.
' RSPCA 2000 Registered Charity No. 219099. Licensed by Licensing By Design Ltd.
RSPCA Trading Ltd (which covenants all its taxable profits to the RSPCA, Registered Charity No.219099) will receive a minimum of £3,200 from the sale of this product line.
RSPCA name and logo are trademarks of RSPCA used by Egmont World Ltd under licence from RSPCA Trading Ltd. For merchandising information please contact Licensing By Design Ltd.
Published in Great Britain in 2000 by Egmont World Ltd, a division of Egmont Holding Ltd, Deanway Technology Centre, Wilmslow Road, Handforth, Cheshire SK9 3FB
Printed in Italy. ISBN 0 7498 4869 3

£5.99 UK only

Contents

G'DAY! WELCOME TO THE ANIMAL HOSPITAL ANNUAL.

I KNOW THAT YOU'RE LIKE ME. YOU REALLY LOVE ANIMALS.

THEY DEPEND ON US TO LOOK AFTER THEM AND GIVE SO MUCH LOVE YET THEY ASK NOTHING IN RETURN.

YOU'LL MEET A LOT OF ANIMALS IN THIS BOOK - FROM THE TRADITIONAL CUDDLY PETS TO NOT-SO-CUDDLY INSECTS! OF COURSE WE FEEL SAD WHEN WE SEE ANIMALS SUFFERING, SO WE CAN NEVER SAY A BIG ENOUGH THANK YOU TO ALL THE RSPCA STAFF ACROSS THE COUNTRY WHO DO SO MUCH FOR ANIMALS IN NEED.

FIND OUT MORE ABOUT THEIR WORK IN THIS BOOK AND COME BEHIND THE SCENES AT THE PUTNEY RSPCA ANIMAL HOSPITAL (WHERE SOME OF THE PROGRAMME HAS BEEN FILMED) TO MEET THE VETS, NURSES AND PATIENTS.

LOOK OUT FOR HELPFUL TIPS ON HOW TO BE A BETTER PET OWNER, AND IF YOU HAVE A CELEBRATION COMING UP WHY NOT ADOPT AN 'ANIMAL THEME' AND HAVE FUN MAKING FOODS SHAPED AS ALL DIFFERENT KINDS OF ANIMALS. IF YOU'RE LIKE ME, AND LOVE TO DRAW, BE CREATIVE BY MAKING YOUR OWN CHRISTMAS CARDS THIS YEAR.

REMEMBER THAT ALL ANIMALS ARE IMPORTANT - BIG AND SMALL. FIND OUT ABOUT THE CREATURES THAT SHARE YOUR HOUSE AND GARDEN. AND SPARE A SEASONAL THOUGHT FOR THE WILDLIFE IN YOUR NEIGHBOURHOOD.

ABOVE ALL, KEEP UP THE GOOD WORK! BE A TRUE ANIMAL LOVER AND FRIEND OF ANIMAL HOSPITAL AND KEEP ON CARING.

SIGNED

NEWS. . . NEWS. . . NEWS. . .

The good news is that millions and millions of viewers are tuning in to **Animal Hospital** each week!

The sad news from **Animal Hospital** is that in the homes of every town and city in the United Kingdom, animals are still suffering because of ignorance and neglect.

We all know that some stories don't have a happy ending. But that is what **Animal Hospital** is all about - real life. Remember that what you see on your screen each week is happening in YOUR town too.

We all want to follow the real-life action as Rolf, Rhodri and Christa report on the everyday happenings at the RSPCA **Animal Hospital**. We all love to join in the excitement as the RSPCA inspectors rush to rescue animals in danger.

We all watch, sometimes stunned, when we see the sad state of the animals brought into the vets' clinics and, of course, we always hope for a happy ending.

If we need proof that **Animal Hospital** is tops - here it is!

Once again, for the fourth year, you, the viewers, voted it The Most Popular Factual Entertainment Programme in the National TV Awards.

Well done, **Animal Hospital**!

Luckily, thanks to the RSPCA there is always someone ready, 24 hours a day, to help.

ROLF SAYS:

"I've been with **Animal Hospital** since the very beginning - 1994. I love the programme because I'm just like the viewers, I never know what'll come through the door.

Each story is a cliff-hanger.....what will happen with the little dog's leg?, or what will the cat's blood test show? The programme is wonderful because it lets us know that it's ok for us to show our feelings.

The series runs for twelve weeks and I spend about three days each week filming. There have been some very sad cases this year - like the tortoise that survived when a hungry fox dug him up from hibernation and tried to eat him - and some remarkable ones - like the 3.6 metre python that hadn't been fed for 6 months, and still made it.

I remember a remarkable operation Chief Vet Tessa Bailey carried out on a road traffic accident cat. His diaphragm had been split by the force of the impact from a car, and Tessa was able to get all his organs back in the right place, stitch him up, and he was back home playing within 4 days.

Animals really are incredible!"

RHODRI SAYS:

"I joined **Animal Hospital** for the Roadshow in May '98. I've covered some pretty amazing stories in the past year. One that sticks in my mind is a swan rescue. I went with RSPCA Animal Collection Officer Christine Graham. It was her first real rescue since qualifying. But she didn't hesitate. She waded into this really fierce water flowing into a storm drain and rescued all the swans. It was great just to be there. Another case I'll never forget was when I went with Inspector Mark Miles to rescue a cat called Turpin who had accidentally been sealed up inside the roof of a house. The builders weren't too happy when we had to rip down part of the roof they had just put up! But the owner was so delighted she burst into song - I think it was: "When Irish Eyes Are Smiling!"

CHRISTA SAYS:

"I'm quite new to **Animal Hospital**. I started in autumn '99 and I really love working as part of the team. I go out with the RSPCA inspectors and animal collection officers to cover stories as they come in. It's very exciting as everything happens so fast! I have to be ready to zoom off at a moment's notice! So far I haven't seen anything too upsetting. I grew up on a farm so I'm quite used to animals. I'll always remember the first time I held a snake - it was a Mexican King snake. I expected it to be cold and slimy but it was quite warm and smooth! There was one creature I just couldn't touch - an escaped tarantula which we took to London Zoo.

RSPCA Putney Animal Hospital

Animal Hospital has been filmed at a number of the RSPCA's domestic animal hospitals, including Harmsworth and Manchester. This book looks at the work of one of those hospitals – in Putney, London.

The RSPCA Putney Animal Hospital cares for sick and injured animals in south London.

There are also two RSPCA-funded outpatient clinics in Camberwell and Ealing.

There are 6 vets and 20 nurses on duty every day.

There has been an animal hospital on the present site in Putney since the 1930s, originally in an old Georgian house.

The patients who come through the hospital doors might be domestic animals brought in by owners who otherwise could not afford veterinary treatment, or injured or abandoned wild animals brought in by RSPCA inspectors and animal collection officers.

The present building was built in 1972 using donations given to the RSPCA, which is the largest animal welfare organisation in the world.

The hospital has several wards where sick animals are cared for day and night - the dog ward, the cat ward, the maternity ward for expectant mothers and the wildlife ward, which is home to anything from a fox to a ferret and a snake to a seagull!

Opening hours are 8.30am – 4.00pm, with clinics dealing with a stream of sick and injured animals. Surgical cases are dealt with in the "fully equipped" operating theatres.

The hospital is staffed 24 hours a day with a vet on call at nights for emergencies.

Of the 20 veterinary nurses at the hospital, 10 are qualified or are students in training and 10 are hospital assistants.

The hospital is headed by hospital director, Tessa Bailey.

The staff on duty might treat up to 100 cases in ONE DAY!

Meet the Putney People

TESSA BAILEY - HOSPITAL DIRECTOR

Tessa, whose face you may recognise from Animal Hospital, has been hospital director at Putney for 8 years. As well as managing the hospital and all its staff, Tessa deals with daily clinics and surgery. She is a specialist in laboratory work, examining cell samples. But her love for animals doesn't stop there! When she leaves the hospital at night, she goes home to an ever-changing family of foster pets which she hand rears, sometimes waking up several times a night to feed hungry babies! At the moment she has 3 cats, 1 dog, 2 rabbits, 1 kitten, 2 grown-up guinea pigs and 3 hand-reared guinea pigs!

DEBBIE CLARKE - HOSPITAL MANAGER

Debbie's job is to make sure that everything in the hospital runs like clockwork! She's responsible for everything from staff training to health and safety. One minute she's planning budgets, the next it's the Christmas fair. But she did sit still long enough to have her photo taken!

DI SHARPE - ASSISTANT MANAGER

Di Sharpe is assistant manager of Putney Hospital and also a qualified veterinary nurse. She has a special companion to keep her calm in times of stress – a lovely Norfolk Terrier cross called Sindy! Di fell in love with Sindy when she was brought into the RSPCA Animal Centre in Chobham by an elderly couple who already had 8 dogs. Di and Sindy have been inseparable ever since.

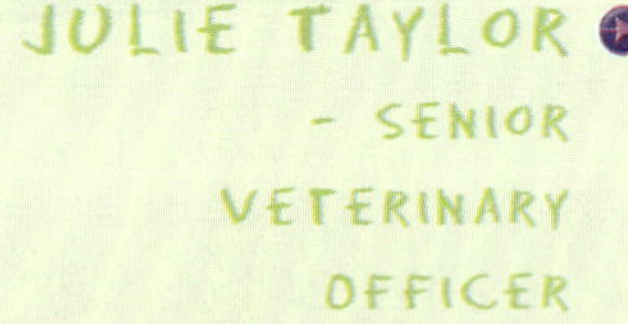

JULIE TAYLOR - SENIOR VETERINARY OFFICER

Julie has been at Putney for 4 years and her time is divided between treating patients in clinics and carrying out surgery in theatre. She knew she wanted to become a vet at the age of 8!

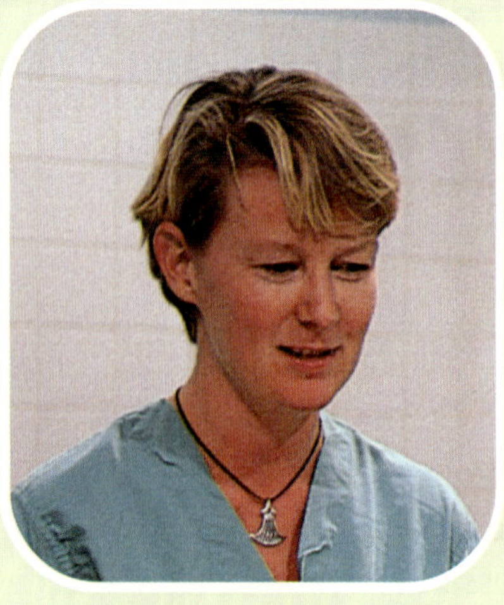

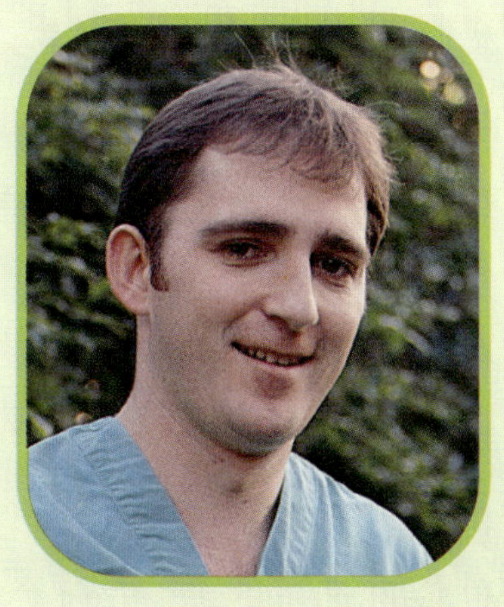

Adam Tjolle - Vet

Adam's is another face you will recognise from your TV screen. A typical day for Adam, or any of the 6 vets who work in the hospital, begins at 8.30am and ends at 5pm. Then, once a week, Adam is on night duty, on call from 8.30am one morning right through the night until 8.30am the following morning! He is allowed to relax, watch TV and sleep, provided he's ready to spring into action the moment the phone rings. Since appearing on Animal Hospital, Adam has become quite well known, but he has one fan who follows him everywhere - a beautiful springer spaniel called Meg. Adam adopted Meg when she was brought to Putney with a broken leg.

Catherine Goulter - Veterinary Nurse

You can identify the different kinds of nurses by the colour of their uniform – green means a qualified veterinary nurse, green stripes mean a student veterinary nurse. Light blue is worn by hospital assistants and dark blue by staff nurses.

All nurses assist the vets in clinics and surgery and also care for the patients on the wards. They are also qualified to do minor surgery and give vaccinations.

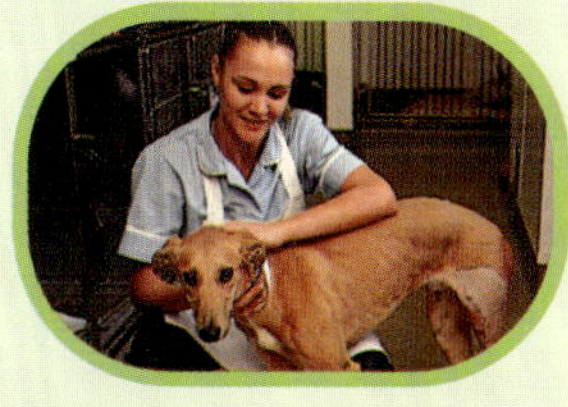

Joolz Smith - Hospital Assistant

There are 10 hospital assistants working at Putney and they are trained to carry out many of the same tasks as the qualified nurses. Many join the hospital straight from school and all must prove that they have a true love of animals. Hospital assistants do all their training at the hospital and work overnight shifts. They are responsible for the care of the patients before and after surgery and assist the vets during clinics.

Pauline Beniston - ACO (Animal Collection Officer)

These RSPCA officers play a vital role in the hospital's work. Their job is to respond to calls which come into the RSPCA's regional communication centres, driving out to tend to injured, abandoned or neglected animals – taking them safely to the hospital for treatment if required, or to an RSPCA animal centre.

Mark Buggie - RSPCA Inspector

Mark Buggie is a popular character at Putney Animal Hospital. He has been with the RSPCA for 10 years and has dealt with almost every kind of case you can imagine! He is one of 14 RSPCA inspectors covering south-east London. Their role is to investigate and, if necessary, prosecute cases of animal cruelty and neglect. Mark is no longer surprised to find 30 cats in a one-bedroomed flat or a box of puppies abandoned on the motorway.

Dogs... Up Close

- People have been keeping dogs as pets for over 10,000 years!
- **Dogs belong to a family of mammals called canids - directly descended from wolves.**
- Every year the RSPCA finds new homes for over 27,000 dogs.
- **The smallest lap dogs only weigh 680 grams!**
- Huge working dogs can weigh up to 90 kilograms!
- **Large dogs are fully mature at the age of 2 and can live to be 18.**
- Small dogs mature earlier at 12 months.
- **Dogs have a third eyelid to keep their eyes clean.**
- There are more than 140 recognised breeds of dog – how many can you name?

THE GOOD DOG OWNER'S CHECKLIST

HOW MANY CAN YOU TICK?

- [ ] I exercise my dog every day.
- [ ] I give my dog a varied diet and plenty of fresh water.
- [ ] My dog is never left alone for long periods.
- [ ] I groom my dog regularly.
- [ ] I train and discipline my dog.
- [ ] I have never left my dog in a car.
- [ ] I take my dog to the vet regularly to be checked, wormed and vaccinated.
- [ ] I am my dog's best friend.

Bags of Doggie Puzzles

How many words beginning with DOG can you recognise?

dog-_ _ _ _ _ ... battered and worn
dog_ _ _ _ ... a small shark
dog_ _ _ _ _ ... where you go when you've been bad
dog_ _ _ ... sharp corner on a race track
dog_ _ _ _ _ ... opinionated and arrogant
dog_ _ ... religious code of beliefs
dog _ _ _ _ _ _ ... first swimming stroke
dogs_ _ _ _ ... person who does all the chores
dog_ _ _ ... very determined

Unscramble the letters in this dog collar to reveal some very famous doggy names!

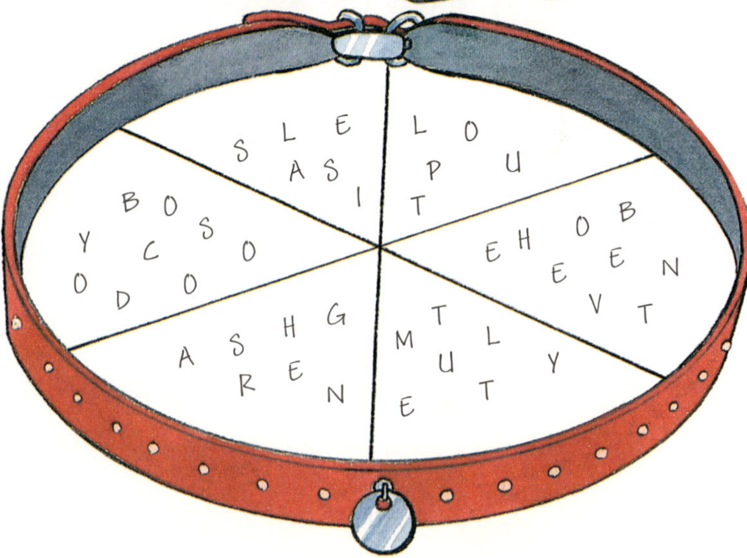

There are 10 different breeds of dog hidden in this word square. Can you find them all?

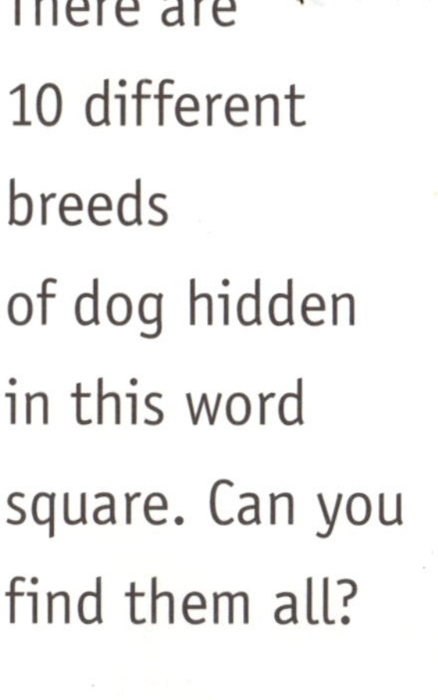

C	H	L	A	B	R	A	D	O	R
O	P	O	O	D	L	E	S	G	D
R	C	O	L	L	I	E	H	R	A
G	H	J	M	N	S	S	E	E	L
I	V	B	K	L	X	T	E	Y	M
X	S	D	F	G	E	E	P	H	A
H	U	S	K	Y	I	G	D	O	T
T	U	E	G	V	F	F	O	U	I
S	P	A	N	I	E	L	G	N	O
A	L	S	A	T	I	A	N	D	N

See page 61 for the answers

The RSPCA - and YOU!

- The RSPCA officially began in 1824. Queen Victoria gave the royal seal of approval to the SPCA - the Society for the Prevention of Cruelty to Animals in 1840.
- **Today the RSPCA has 328 inspectors investigating over 130,000 complaints of cruelty to animals each year in England and Wales.**
- RSPCA animal hospitals and clinics in England and Wales treat over 275,000 cases a year and find homes for 100,000 animals.
- **In the past year alone, more than 1.5 million people have called the RSPCA.**
- There are 194 local RSPCA branches across the country and 49 animal re-homing centres.
- **There are 4 RSPCA domestic animal hospitals in England: 2 are in London (Putney and Harmsworth), 1 is in Birmingham and 1 in Manchester. And there are 3 wildlife hospitals: 1 in Norfolk, 1 in Cheshire and 1 in Somerset.** **(Turn to page 44 for a special report from the RSPCA Stapeley Grange Wildlife Hospital.)**

HOW YOU CAN HELP

- Tell the RSPCA about an injured animal or animal being mistreated by calling their 24-hour national cruelty line: 0870 55 55 999.
- **Support the RSPCA's campaign to clean up our streets and countryside. Litter and rubbish cause a real threat to wildlife and animals. Take your bottles, cans and newspapers to your local recycling depot.**
- Have your pet microchipped! It's easy and safe. A tiny microchip, the size of a grain of rice, is inserted under your pet's skin. It will cost about £20 at your local veterinary centre. But once it is done, your pet is tagged for life and your details can easily be amended if you move house. More than 600,000 animals (mainly cats, dogs and horses) have been microchipped in the past five years - make sure your pet joins them.
- **Be a responsible pet owner and have your pet neutered. This is a simple operation to avoid unwanted pregnancy. Your pet will recover quickly and lead a happier, healthier life. Females are 'spayed' and males are 'castrated'. Your vet will tell you the best age for this to be done.**

- Help your nearest RSPCA branch with their work.

Animals All Year Round

SPRING TIME...

... is baby boom time!

Fledglings take their first flight and young cubs scamper bravely into the big wide world.

If you see a baby animal apparently abandoned, please don't be tempted to rescue it! Leave it where it is. Usually the parents are close by but out of sight. You should only encourage the baby to move to a safer spot if you think it is in danger. Only contact the RSPCA if you are sure it is injured. Never try to look after a baby animal yourself – it will need expert attention if it is to survive.

SUMMER TIME...

... is thirsty work!

Give your pet plenty of fresh water and never, ever leave it in a car – in hot weather an animal can die within minutes. Check your pet regularly for mites and fleas which thrive in warm weather.

If you're off on holiday, don't forget your pet! Choose a good kennel or cattery or ask a reliable neighbour or friend to look after your pet while you are away.

Cats do prefer to stay in their own home, and someone would need to visit at least twice a day. Fish, caged birds and other animals can be looked after by trusted friends.

Summer is also time for fairs, fêtés and circuses. If you see a stall offering goldfish as a prize – don't play the game! Pets are a big responsibility – not a spur-of-the-moment thing. Many goldfish die soon after you get them home because of stress, oxygen starvation or changes in water temperature and quality.

AUTUMN TIME...

... is noisy!

Remember, remember the fifth of November. But remember to keep your pet indoors and well away from loud fireworks. Just in case the worst happens and your pet does get startled and run away – have it microchipped now!

If you are building a bonfire make sure no unsuspecting creatures have burrowed inside thinking it is a convenient winter home! Watch out especially for hedgehogs which are looking for somewhere to hibernate. Hedgehogs need to put on weight to survive the winter. You can help by feeding them minced meat, tinned dog food or scrambled egg mixed with crushed dog biscuits. Make sure you leave out fresh water too. Hedgehogs are useful garden visitors as they eat slugs.

WINTER TIME...

... is cold and bare!

Food is scarce now and you might find all kinds of wildlife wandering into your garden.

Leave plenty of scraps out for the birds - stale cake, grated cheese, cooked rice, moist breadcrumbs and bacon rind will fill empty tummies during the cold months. Remember to leave out fresh water to drink and bathe in, as ponds and lakes are frozen over.

Wrap up warm and visit your local pond – few people bother in winter. Take some moist bread or finely chopped lettuce or cabbage to give the ducks a winter treat.

Put pets in outside cages into a garage or shed and give them extra bedding.

It gets dark early - so give your dog or cat a reflective collar for Christmas to make sure it can be seen!

PIN-UP PETS!

You all think your pets are gorgeous, and here's the proof – a gallery of perfect pin-ups.

West Byfleet
Surrey

Dear Animal Hopital
I am Learning about letters at school and I would like to a few questions on animals.
What is your favourite animal, mine Is a dog. I would like to have my own pet but I havn't got one at all.
What is the most unusual you have had In the building.
How many animals come to the vet a year
Whhat Is the best thing about working with animals and why.
I would really like a reply.
Yours faithfully
Abigail

Rolf with a dog
Lewis

Leeds

Jenny Burt

hello Rolf

TWEET TWEET

Surrey.

Dear Rolf
I am going to work with you when I grow up.
Love from
Lewis Smith (Age 5)

I have two Kitten's this is my one tigger.

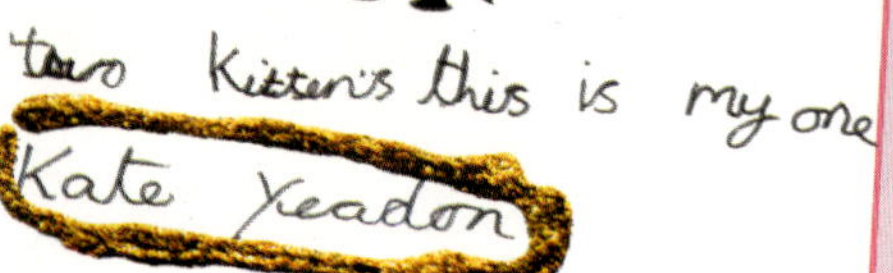

West Byfleet Junior School

West Byfleet,
Surrey
Kt 14 6EF.

Samantha.A.morris

West Sussex

Lucy is a white pony that I ride and Samantha rides a black pony called Daisy.

Love from Ethel Jennifer Martin Joanne Susan Janice Flaudie Samantha

St Francis School.
Nailsea
North Somerset

To Rolf
I Love your programe
I have 4 cats called oscar
Josh and Rosie and Phardon
I have 2 Rabbits called
Daisy and Tulip
Love
from Shannon Savage
age 6.

Luton,
Beds

Dear Rolf,

I had to write to you to tell you about my Little Goddaughter Claire, she is 4 years old but when she was born she was only 1lb 10oz so as you could imagine she is very special & very petite. Her Mum and I took her to see Father Christmas on Sunday he asked her what she wanted for Christmas and to everyone's surprise she said "Rolf Harris" & 3 hairbands Father Christmas & his Elf just couldn't stop Laughing.

Thankyou for making us all have such a good Laugh!

Love
Linda Goldie (mrs).

Cambridge
CB5 8PJ

Dear Rolf harris

Hello, my name is Sarah Brown. I am 12 years old and I Love animals.

All my Family Like you and we all watch your Show animal hospital. I have a Dog Called Sadie and 2 cats called Star and Smudge. They Live round my dads. I have a Pet bird called Charlie and Shes Laid 4 eggs. I also have some sea monkeys. I used to have a hampster called bubbles but She died of a tuma. I am still really upset about her. but I am getting a new hamster Soon.

your Dog Summer.

Thank you
and Take care
Love From
Sarah
·X·X·X·X·X·

Putney Animal Hospital - Real Life On the Wards

Come behind the scenes now to look at the work of the RSPCA Putney Animal Hospital. Each patient has a special story to tell...

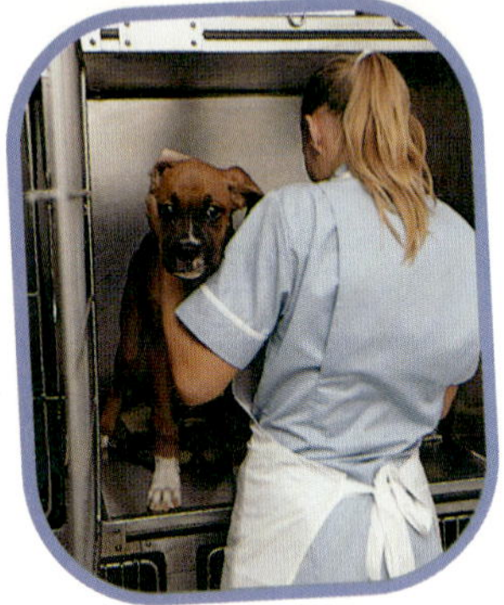

THE DOG WARD

Lisa Moore is on duty today in the dog ward. Most of the cages here are occupied. Some patients look quite poorly and are waiting for surgery. Others have already had their operations and are coming round from the anaesthetic. One dog is noisily growling in his sleep. Twice a day those that are well enough are allowed out to exercise in the runs while their cages are cleaned and disinfected. Lisa must keep a close eye on each patient. She will give each one all the expert care and attention it needs to get well.

In one cage is a beautiful white German shepherd. She is only young and looks quite sorry for herself with her heavily bandaged leg. She was brought to the hospital ten days ago after she was seen being knocked down by a car. The driver never stopped, but a kind passer-by reported the accident. When she was examined the vet was shocked by the deep wounds to her leg and now she faces several weeks of dressings until they heal. Lisa says she has a lovely temperament and although no one has claimed her yet, they are hopeful that somewhere her owner has realised she has strayed and may contact the hospital. If not, when she is well again she will be taken to Battersea Dogs' Home...

*******If this patient had been microchipped she would soon be going home. Turn to page 15 to find out more.***

Along the row of cages, past sleeping neighbours, we find another young dog with an injured back leg. She is a lurcher with lovely brown eyes. She has been sent from Battersea Dogs' Home for urgent surgery. She too has been hit by a car and the vets have discovered that part of her femur (thighbone) has completely snapped off and will never heal. They must therefore operate to remove the piece of broken bone. But right now her leg is too sore for any more surgery. She can't walk on it at all, but hobbles eagerly to nurse Joolz Smith when her cage door is opened. The vets are hopeful that with the piece of bone taken out, her leg will heal. Then she will join the other homeless dogs back at Battersea Dogs' Home and hope that someone somewhere will give her the happy home that she deserves...

PS. Her operation was a success and she was transferred back to Battersea Dogs' Home.

THE CAT WARD

Further along the corridor, behind another door at Putney, we find ourselves on the cat ward. Here the little cages are filled with soft, furry felines. There is no noise – a sure sign that these patients are not well. Today Catherine Goulter is the veterinary nurse on duty. She reads the notes pinned to each cage door and stops to open one to check on a beautiful stray who was brought in after a road accident. He appears well enough but Catherine explains that the accident has caused internal injuries which make it difficult for him to control his bladder. She strokes him and he starts to purr loudly. But his condition is quite serious. When the car hit him it may have caused irreparable nerve damage, for which there is no cure. Sadly, if the nerves don't heal, this patient will not survive. But for now, he is eating well - and purring very loudly! What's more, the 'finder' who brought him in after the accident wants to give him a home - so this looks like a story with a happy ending...

PS. Two weeks later he was fully recovered and went to his new home.

In the next cage is a very strange-looking cat – who happens to be a puppy! Catherine explains that he is here not only because he is so small, but also because he hasn't yet been vaccinated. He must be separated from the other dogs in the main dog ward in case of infection. It is quite safe for him to be here, as cats cannot catch infections from dogs. His name is Pepsi and he's 4 months old. All puppies like to chew things – but this one went too far and bit the end off a baby's dummy, then swallowed it! The vets had to do an emergency operation to remove the piece of rubber from inside Pepsi, but now he's lively and recovering well and due to go home in a few days' time.

As we leave the cat ward and close the door behind us we think how lucky our own pets are to be safe and well at home.

THE WILDLIFE WARD

If you thought it strange to find a dog in the cat ward, take a look inside this ward – and you'll be amazed! This is the wildlife ward, where you really must expect the unexpected! Here is a whole menagerie of animals!

Today the list of residents reads like this:

- ONE FRIGHTENED FOX, HIDING BEHIND A SHEET
- TWO FRANTIC FERRETS IN NEED OF FLUIDS
- ONE LAZY BLUE-TONGUED LIZARD (RESCUED FROM BENEATH SOMEONE'S SETTEE!)
- ONE BABY HERRING GULL
- THREE BEWILDERED BIRDS
- TWO RASCALLY RABBITS AND
- ONE RUNAWAY RAT!

As you can imagine, the nurses working here have to be prepared for anything!

The shelves are packed with plastic boxes of food, all neatly labelled, along with plenty of reference books to check up on the patients' requirements. Today's main question is: What does a blue-tongued lizard like to eat?

The staff have to be quick-witted and know how to improvise! The lizard is in a temperature-controlled vivarium. The nervous fox is hidden away from bright lights with a sheet. The birds have their own special cages and the ferrets are given plenty of room to run about but away from their natural prey, such as rabbits.

Once these patients have recovered, the staff must contact one of the many specialist wildlife or re-homing centres around the country. Here, with expert care and attention, even the rarest of animals can be found the right home and native wild animals can be released back into their natural habitat. The work of these centres is vital. Without them the future for these little patients would be very bleak. ***(You can read all about one RSPCA wildlife centre on page 44.)***

THE PREP ROOM

Walk through a heavy set of swing doors and you are inside the 'prep' room. This is where patients are prepared for surgery. Jennie Nicholas is staff nurse in charge of the operating theatres. Today she is helping the vet to anaesthetise a very large grey rabbit called Fat Boy! He is about to have some dental surgery and has been given the first of two special injections which will put him safely to sleep for his operation...

THE MATERNITY WARD

The last ward we visit is the maternity ward. The only residents here today are two six-week-old feral kittens, found abandoned in a box in Wembley Stadium, and brought to the hospital by the RSPCA animal collection officers. This time we think pictures speak louder than words!

*******The wild and stray cat population is exploding! You can help by being a responsible cat owner and having your cat neutered. See page 15 for more details.***

Time Out to ...COOK!

Here's some party-animal food that's lots of fun to make!
But, remember: children should be supervised by an adult when cooking.

CRUNCHY CATERPILLAR

You will need:
one large cucumber
small bunch of green grapes
small bunch of red grapes
cocktail sticks
2 glacé cherries

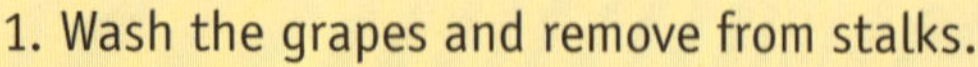

1. Wash the grapes and remove from stalks.
2. Put each grape on to a cocktail stick.
3. Stick the other end of the cocktail stick into the cucumber and arrange in a coloured pattern along the length of your 'caterpillar'.
4. Use two more cocktail sticks to give the caterpillar glacé-cherry eyes!

HEALTHY HEDGEHOG

You will need:
one grapefruit
cheddar cheese
raisins
cocktail sticks
two glacé cherries

1. Cut the grapefruit in half.
2. Place the grapefruit flat-side down.
3. Cut cheese into cubes and arrange on cocktail sticks with the raisins.
4. Stick the 'spines' on to the hedgehog.
5. Give your hedgehog two red eyes!

CRUNCHY COOKIES

To make about 15 biscuits, you will need:
125g softened butter or margarine
1 beaten egg
125g caster sugar
175g sifted plain flour
3 tablespoons cocoa powder
animal-shaped cutters
greased baking tray

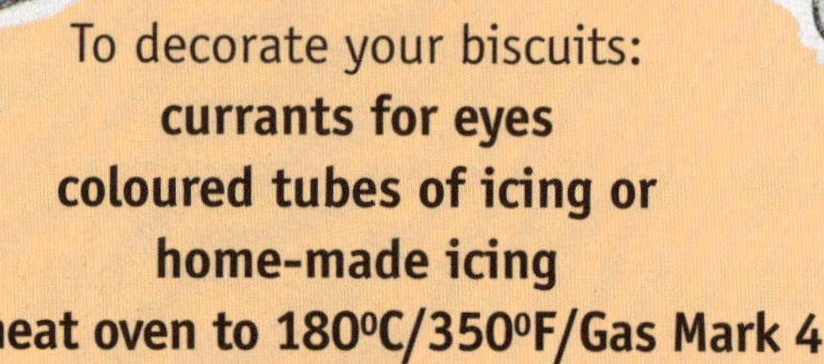

To decorate your biscuits:
currants for eyes
coloured tubes of icing or
home-made icing
Pre-heat oven to 180°C/350°F/Gas Mark 4

1. Mix the sugar and butter in a bowl.
2. Stir in the beaten egg a little at a time.
3. Stir in the sifted flour and cocoa powder.
4. Use your hands to mix the dough into a ball.
5. Wrap the dough in cling film and place in the fridge for 30 minutes or the freezer for 10 minutes.
6. Roll out the dough on a floury surface.
7. Use your shaped cutter and place the biscuits on to your baking tray.
8. Add eyes to your animals using currants.
9. Bake for 10 minutes and cool on a wire rack.
10. Decorate your animals using coloured tubes of icing, or make your own icing with icing sugar, warm water and food colour.

SAVOURY SNAKES

You will need:

150g self-raising flour
½ teaspoon salt
25g margarine
85g grated cheese
1 egg and 2 tablespoons of milk mixed together
raisins for eyes
strips of red and green pepper or slices of baby tomatoes to decorate
greased baking tray

1. Sift the flour and salt together.
2. Add margarine and rub together using your fingertips.
3. Leave 1 tablespoon of cheese aside. Add the rest to the mixture.
4. Leave 1 tablespoon of milk and egg mixture aside. Add the rest to the mixture.
5. Mix the dough together and roll out on a floury surface.
6. Cut the dough into snake shapes. Press one end flat for the head.
7. Brush the snakes with the left-over egg mixture and sprinkle with the left-over cheese.
8. Add raisins for eyes.
9. Decorate with strips of red and green pepper or small slices of tomato.
10. Place onto a greased baking tray and bake for about 8-10 minutes.

MOUSEY PIZZA

You will need:

290g packet of pizza base mix or ready-to-cook pizza base
flour for sprinkling
small jar of tomato pizza topping
4 baby tomatoes
150g grated mozzarella cheese
8 black olives

1. Grease a large baking sheet and pre-heat the oven to 200°C/ 425°F /Gas Mark 7.
2. Make up the pizza mix following the instructions on the packet.
3. Roll out into a circle or place your ready-made pizza base on to a floured surface.
4. Cut the pizza into quarters.
5. Spread each quarter with tomato pizza topping.
6. Sprinkle with cheese.
7. Add the mice ears by cutting small triangles of tomato.
8. Give the mice eyes with black olives.
9. Make noses from the remaining tomato.
10. Bake in the oven for about 10-12 minutes.

WORK, WORK, WORK...

If you're a regular viewer of **Animal Hospital**, you'll know that working with animals is not all fun!

Do you think you might be cut out to work with animals? Then take a trip along this road and see where it takes you...

Congratulations!
You have what it takes to work with animals!

YOU STILL HAVE LOTS OF TIME TO THINK ABOUT YOUR CAREER, SO HERE ARE SOME WORDS OF WISDOM TO HELP YOU...

"It is vital to have some practical experience to find out if you really like working with animals. The first two years after you qualify can be very stressful. Then you gain confidence, but as a vet you are always learning. And remember - you don't only treat fluffy pets!"

(TESSA BAILEY)

"Being a vet involves hard work and long hours and can be upsetting. Every day you are dealing with life and death. You have to be tough and the worst part is seeing all the stray animals who just can't be housed."

(SARAH THOMAS)

"We may see up to 100 patients a day! It's very stressful. People can sit in the waiting room for 3 hours and then we only have a matter of minutes to deal with them. As a vet you want to give your best to each patient and the hardest thing is when you realise you can't do any more to help. But the work is wonderfully challenging – and rewarding too, when someone you have helped says thank you."

(JULIE TAYLOR)

"I first knew I wanted to be a vet at the age of 7. I didn't get the right grades first time around, so I kept trying until I did. Choosing to be a vet is a vocation."

(ADAM TJOLLE)

Hamsters... Up Close

• All pet hamsters originate from just two females and one male captured in Syria in 1930!

• Hamsters are classed as rodents with food-carrying cheek pouches.

• Hamsters live an average of 2 years.

• The female is only pregnant for 16 days but can have up to 18 babies!

• Some hamsters grow to be 30 cm (12 inches) long!

• In the wild, hamsters live in underground burrows.

• Their natural habitat is in the plains and deserts of Asia.

***** If your hamster escapes, try this. Put some soft bedding and tasty nibbles in the bottom of a bucket. Place a ladder against the bucket (a wire rack from the oven will do). Place a trail of food at the foot of the ladder. Leave overnight and in the morning you should find your adventurous friend has come home!*

THE GOOD HAMSTER OWNER'S CHECKLIST

HOW MANY CAN YOU TICK?

- [ ] I have the patience to make friends with my hamster.
- [ ] I understand that my pet prefers to sleep during the day.
- [ ] My hamster's cage is completely safe (they can escape through the tiniest hole).
- [ ] I clean out the cage regularly.
- [ ] My pet has some hard wood for gnawing.
- [ ] I give my pet a mixed diet, including fresh fruit and vegetables.
- [ ] I keep my pet warm so he doesn't hibernate.
- [ ] My pet has lots of tunnels and toys to play with.
- [ ] I will be my pet's best friend for life.

Puzzles to Get Your Teeth Into!

Hamster isn't the only word to begin with the letters HAM. Can you guess these? Look at the pictures for clues.

ham_ _ _ _ _ _
ham_ _ _
ham_ _ _ _
ham_ _ _
ham s_ _ _ _ _ _ _

This hamster wants to get to his food store – can you show him the QUICKEST way?

Find the letters that appear ONLY ONCE in this grid to spell a hamster's favourite nibble!

A	Y	D	F	D	A	E	R	K
A	D	R	G	H	J	F	H	L
G	H	N	M	K	H	J	H	G
D	F	G	U	R	R	D	F	G
B	V	B	K	T	A	L	J	H
B	A	A	R	Y	S	A	D	A
A	M	E	G	V	F	K	A	V
D	J	K	B	E	K	V	F	V
F	G	Y	H	D	M	F	K	H

See page 61 for the answers

Time Out to ...DRAW

There's a real art to drawing animals! If you've ever tried you'll know how difficult it can be. So here are some tips from the experts on how to make your animal drawings more life like!

A Prickly Tale

Katie was bored. Saturday morning TV had finished and it was raining. Having an older brother didn't help. He was always out doing stuff - playing football or meeting his friends. She tipped her bag of Barbie clothes on to the bedroom floor. Then emptied her box of farmyard animals on top.

Boring, boring. Her life was so boring.

Her dad was in the kitchen creating a delicious garlicky smell. He was the best cook in the world. She ran over and gave him a hug.

"Watch out!" he laughed, holding up two floury white hands.

She heard a key turn in the front door. Her mum came in, dropping her heavy briefcase on the stairs.

"You look fed up," she said, seeing Katie's gloomy face in the doorway. "Why don't you call next door and see if they can play for half an hour before lunch - smells like it's nearly ready!"

Good thinking! Katie slipped on her sandals, even though it was raining, and pulled her fleece from the hook. The boys next door would have something to do.

She ran round in the rain. Sam and Jack's house was so much more interesting than her own. They lived with their mum who was kind, a crazy dog called Sally, a three-legged cat called Charlie, two rabbits who ran about the house and a hamster who lived in a maze of tunnels.

She pressed the door bell. It made a kind of flat buzz. Someone was playing the piano. After about a minute (which was usual) the music stopped, a voice shouted, footsteps thundered down the stairs, and Sam opened the door. He was 10, with curly hair, green eyes and a cheeky smile and, although he was sometimes naughty, he was fun.

"Hi, Sam," she smiled.

"Hi, Katie. Shall we play out? Jack's doing his homework."

"It's raining..."

"So?"

Sally the dog rushed past them into the garden.

"Let's go to the Wendy House," grinned Sam.

Even Sam's garden was more interesting than hers. It went uphill behind their house to two great climbing trees, an apple and a pear. In the summer they could spend hours sitting in the branches. One tree had a swing seat and rope ladder and the other had a broken-down tree house. Tucked into one corner of the garden, almost hidden behind a huge overgrown hedge, was an old Wendy House which gave Katie the creeps. Sam yanked open the wooden door and ducked inside.

Katie followed, sensibly putting on the gloves that she found in the pocket of her fleece. The Wendy House was full of old things - little chairs, a red plastic desk covered in stickers, a blackboard and a toddler's kitchen with pretend food, all covered in cobwebs. On the floor was a piece of old carpet that was brown and mouldy where the rain seeped in. Sam picked up a plastic sausage and started poking the biggest cobwebs. Katie peered out through the little window and noticed Sally, the dog, digging frantically in the compost heap.

"Should Sally be doing that?" she wondered out loud.

Sam looked. "Nope."

"Should we stop her?"

"Don't be daft. Looks like she's found buried treasure!"

They both watched as the dog's digging became more and more furious. Compost was flying in all directions. Then suddenly her little brown and white head appeared triumphant! And in her mouth - could it be? Katie and Sam stared hard. It was! A real, live hedgehog!

The children moved with such speed that the dog's moment of triumph was over in a flash. Sam grabbed her collar and yelled, "Sally, drop it!" which the startled dog did more from shock than obedience, while Katie, suddenly grateful for her gloves, lifted the muddy 'treasure' away. She had never touched a hedgehog before. How could a living thing be so fragile and delicate and stiff and spiky all at the same time?

She made for the Wendy House. Sam ran after her, slamming the wooden door behind him, sending spiders running for cover and leaving a bewildered Sally sniffing in the rain.

The children stood motionless for a few seconds, looking at the little creature. Katie hardly dared move.

"It's petrified," said Sam. "But if we put it back, Sally will have it again."

"I bet it was hibernating," said Katie. "They do that. I saw it on Blue Peter."

Sam reached out to touch the spines, making the hedgehog curl up even tighter. "We could make it a bed in here," he suggested. "Then we can keep it safe."

Katie looked at him. She saw his green eyes twinkle with excitement. She thought for a moment. It seemed like a good idea. "OK, then. But let's try and feed it first."

"You wait here," said Sam, excitedly, "and I'll go and find out what they eat." And with that he left Katie and the hedgehog all alone.

Katie hoped that if she kept really still the hedgehog might uncurl itself. She wanted to see its little face. But it was so frightened. She looked at the dense coat of spines, all clogged with bits of mud and leaves. She felt sorry for this little thing. It was so helpless and Sally the dog must have seemed like a terrible monster. She wished she could let it know she would never harm it.

Suddenly Sam burst back into her silence. "Insects, worms, frogs, snakes, mice and birds' eggs!" He rattled off the list he'd been memorising all the way from his bedroom.

"What?!"

"Insects, worms, frogs, snakes, mice and birds' eggs..."

"That's not much help - unless you fancy digging up some worms...!"

Sam looked blank.

Then Katie remembered something. "I think on Blue Peter they said they eat dog food."

"Brilliant!" Sam ran off and returned, not only with a tin of dog food, but also a red toy chest that his action men had been in, a blanket, a dish and two bags of hamster bedding. "Everything a homeless hedgehog could wish for!" he beamed.

As they tucked their new-found friend up, Katie felt a stab of anxiety. "Shouldn't we just let it go?" she asked.

"No way! We're saving its life!" said Sam, his green eyes full of adventure. "Let's give him a name... how about Spike?"

Katie pulled a face. "I think she's a girl and we should call her Compo, because she came out of the compost heap!"

"Agreed! But we must keep this a secret - our secret. OK?"

Katie nodded and they shook hands to seal the promise.

With Compo to think about, Katie didn't have time to get bored. That afternoon she went to the library and found five books that mentioned hedgehogs and read every page - twice. Each day, after school, she met Sam under the apple tree. They'd play for a while, make sure no one was watching, then disappear into the Wendy House. At first Compo would only eat after they had gone. But then, one evening when Katie had brought round some of her dad's best scrambled eggs, a little face peeped cautiously from beneath the blanket. The children held their breath as two black eyes blinked at them, and a long pointed

Saturday lunchtime. Sam pushed the door to the Wendy House and Katie went in first. She couldn't believe her eyes. The pile of chairs was gone. The blackboard, the desk, the kitchen - all gone. The carpet had been taken up and the floor swept. And, her eyes darted about frantically, the red toy chest - was gone too!

"Where is everything?" Sam had rushed inside to where his mother was working at the computer. Katie followed,

"Hmmm?" His mother wasn't really listening.

"Mum. What have you done with all the stuff in the Wendy House?" he repeated in a loud, panicky voice.

"Calm down," she replied, staring at him. "What's the fuss? I had a clear-out. It was in such a mess. Why do you hate me throwing things out?"

Sam exchanged a glance with Katie."What have you done with it all?"

"I recycled it! I gave the good stuff away and took the rest to the tip."

An awful image came into Katie's mind of huge crushing machines and fierce guard dogs.

"What about my red toy chest?" asked Sam, nervously.

nose sniffed its way towards the tasty dish of food.

"Awwhh!" whispered Katie, in a voice barely louder than a sigh.

"Sweet!" mouthed Sam. And they watched as their little visitor tasted the eggs, drank from the bowl of water, and scampered back under the blanket to hide.

From then on Compo would venture out each evening as they watched. She began to recognise their voices - and certainly knew when scrambled eggs were on the menu! Katie felt so happy. She had never had an animal of her own to take care of. She sometimes worried that keeping Compo wasn't really the right thing to do - but then Sally-the-terrible was waiting outside!

Several weeks went by. Everything was going well - until the unthinkable happened. It was a

"Hmmm...let me think," said his mother, not taking her eyes from the screen, "oh yes, I meant to tell you. It was so cute. A lovely little hedgehog had made a nest inside it in one of your old baby blankets! I was going to keep it and show you, but you should never try to keep wild animals - should you?" She glanced at the two rosy-faced children for a second, then carried on with her work. "I set it free in the garden. It seemed very happy to go...".

Nothing was the same now. Katie didn't feel like playing with Sam any more. Weeks passed before she called at his house one night after dinner. She pressed the door bell which rang with its usual flat buzz. Sam stuffed his feet in his trainers and came outside. They wandered up the garden, more from habit than choice, towards the overgrown hedge and pushed the wooden door to the Wendy House. It wasn't creepy anymore, just bare and empty. They sat on the damp floor with nothing to say.

Eventually Katie stood up and peered out through the window.

"Keeping Compo was the best fun I've ever had," she said, "although maybe it was wrong."

"We didn't mean any harm," said Sam, picking up a woodlouse and making it curl into a ball, "And anyway, I still say we saved her life."

He came and stood next to Katie and, as they both stared out into the dark garden, something amazing happened. From out of the bushes came two black eyes and a long, sniffing nose.

Sam grabbed Katie's arm.

"It's Compo!" he hissed in a loud whisper. "I bet she heard our voices!"

"And guess what?" giggled Katie. "We had scrambled eggs for tea!"

Sure enough, later that night, as the children knelt down and pushed the dish towards her, Compo came gratefully across the grass to eat. And when she finished she scuttled back into the dark bushes. Back where she belonged.

Fingerprint Fun!

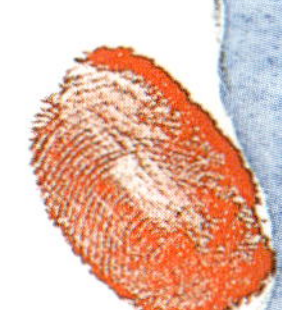

There's nothing nicer than something handmade at Christmas, and this year everything you need is at your fingertips! It's a unique way to wish your friends and family a happy Christmas – cards and gift-tags that are as individual as you are – made with your very own fingerprints!

HERE'S WHAT TO DO:

1. Cut your card according to what you are making. Gift-tags can be any shape – square, circular or star-shaped. Cards must stand up so they need a flat base – choose a square, rectangular or triangular shape.

2. Paint your index finger with washable paint or ink and press your fingerprint onto the card.

YOU WILL NEED:

white, black or coloured card
washable paint or ink
felt-tipped pens

3. Turn your fingerprint into anything you choose! Here are some animal ideas...

Putney Animal Hospital - Real Life In the Clinics

If we look behind the clinic doors at the RSPCA Putney Animal Hospital we find Tessa Bailey and Rolf Harris in the middle of filming for the next edition of **Animal Hospital**. The cameras are rolling, the lights are bright, but the vital work of caring for sick animals continues...

On the table is a big friendly cat called Sammy. He is aged 8 and has a history of problems with nasty lumps in his throat. His owner explains that these make it difficult for Sammy to breathe.

Tessa has some good news. As a result of tests done the previous week, she is certain that the lumps are not cancerous and can be controlled with tablets. She has some advice, too - cats are notoriously fussy eaters and when tablets are hidden in food they often get left behind. Tessa advises crushing the tablet into tiny pieces to make sure it gets eaten. The lumps in Sammy's throat are nodules caused by inflammation. Tessa explains that the tablets she prescribes won't actually cure the lumps but will control them and stop them from spreading. The only other alternative would be surgery to remove the lumps but Tessa says that this isn't really necessary yet. Now Sammy can return home and look forward to feeling better.

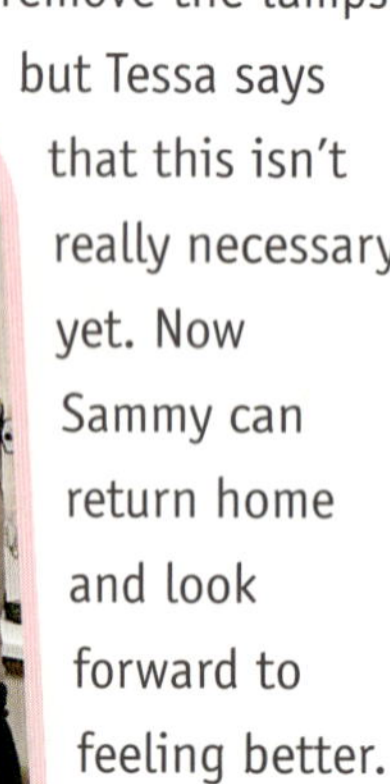

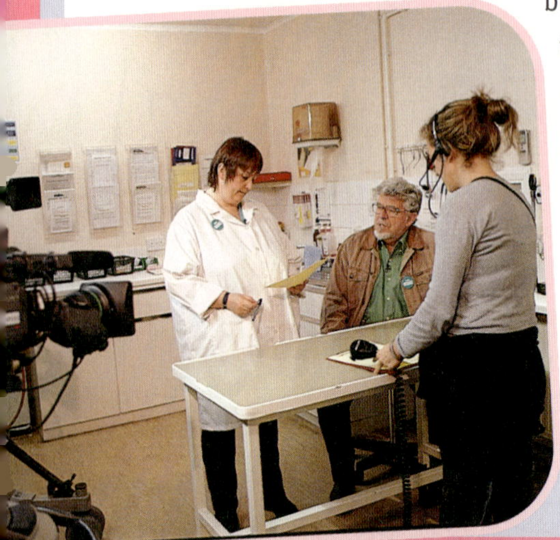

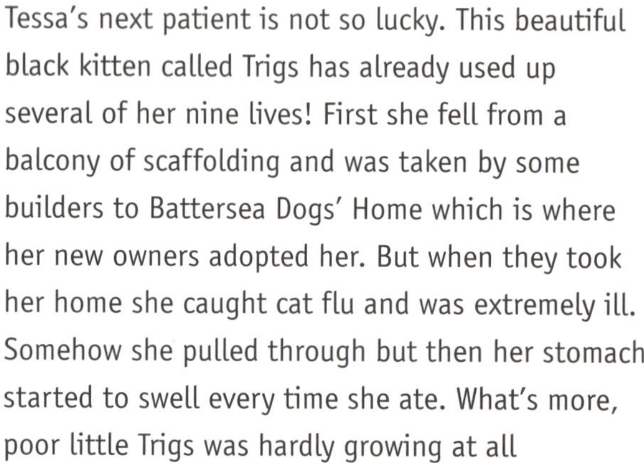

Tessa's next patient is not so lucky. This beautiful black kitten called Trigs has already used up several of her nine lives! First she fell from a balcony of scaffolding and was taken by some builders to Battersea Dogs' Home which is where her new owners adopted her. But when they took her home she caught cat flu and was extremely ill. Somehow she pulled through but then her stomach started to swell every time she ate. What's more, poor little Trigs was hardly growing at all and couldn't use her back legs properly.

Tessa is very concerned. She says that although the kitten is at least 6 months old she is only the size of a kitten 14 weeks old. Tessa listens to her heart very carefully. She can hear something strange. She listens again. She has found a heart murmur - an irregularity in the way the heart is beating and pumping blood around the body. This explains why Trigs is so small and weak. Her heart is not working as well as it should.

The good news is that Trigs doesn't appear to be in any pain. Her owners say she is playful and eating well. Tessa says that an X-ray will be taken and Trigs will be referred to a specialist cardiologist who will prescribe the best treatment for her.

This might be a course of tablets or injections or even surgery. Tessa says that if Trigs was a human patient she would be in need of a heart transplant.

But for now Trigs has the best possible medicine - two owners who love her very much and will do whatever it takes to give her a happy life.

In another room, vet Adam Tjolle is running his clinic. Adam's first patient is a 10-week-old guinea pig called Max. His owner is worried because Max is aggressive - often biting her for no apparent reason. Adam is worried too – he has to lift Max out of the box! Carefully he holds Max behind his neck to keep away from those teeth! Adam explains that it is unusual for a guinea pig to bite, but quickly he diagnoses a very bad case of mange – a skin disease caused by mites. Not only does this make Max feel uncomfortable and bad-tempered, it also means his skin is very sensitive, which is why he bites when he is touched. Adam gives Max an injection to kill the mites and then notices that Max is a male guinea pig. He advises that Max should come back when he is 4 months old to be castrated. This will help to make him less aggressive and help to give him a long and healthy life.

****Turn to page 15 for more advice on neutering your pet.***

Next, Adam calls for Whisky – not the drink, but the cat! His owner explains that Whisky is 20 years old and has only been to the vet once in his whole life! But recently Whisky always seems to be thirsty. Adam examines the cat thoroughly and pronounces him in wonderful health. He explains that at his age his kidneys may be finding it difficult to cope and that this is a natural part of ageing. Whisky is drinking a lot to help his kidneys flush out waste products from his body. Adam prescribes a course of anabolic steroid injections to help keep Whisky happy and healthy for as long as possible.

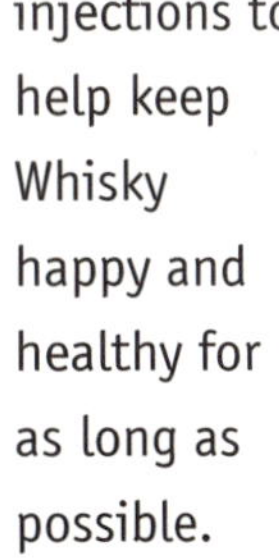

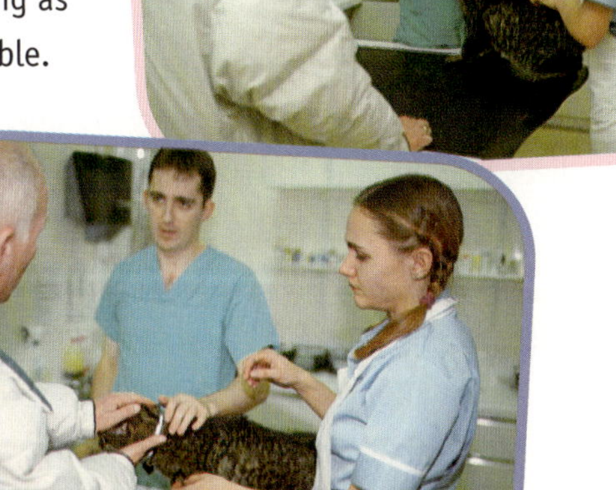

Adam's next patient is definitely NOT getting on to the table! He's called Bubba and he is an 8-month-old bull mastiff who weighs in at 45.1 kilos - and is still growing! Adam guesses that when fully grown he could weigh 80 kilos! His owner has brought him in for the first of two very important injections. These are given to all puppies - usually at around 8 weeks old, with the second follow-up injection at 12 weeks. The injections protect dogs against the five most common canine diseases - hepatitis, distemper, parvovirus, leptospirosis and parainfluenza. Bubba doesn't feel a thing and Adam explains to his owner that, like all dogs, it is important for Bubba to come back for yearly boosters to keep up his protection.

Next on to Adam's table is Tyson – a naughty young Staffy who has chewed and swallowed 12 Ibuprofen tablets! Now his owners are very anxious because Tyson has not eaten for 4 days and is still being sick. Adam is concerned, too. He looks at Tyson's eyes and mouth. He listens to his heart and feels all around his stomach. The tablets he has swallowed may have damaged the lining of his stomach and even his liver or kidneys. Tyson will have to be closely monitored. Adam gives him a tablet to stop the production of acid in his stomach and wants to admit him for X-rays. Dogs like Staffies are often inquisitive and cheeky. It is very important to avoid accidents by being extra-watchful. Hopefully Tyson will recover from this ordeal, but his owners have really learned their lesson the hard way.

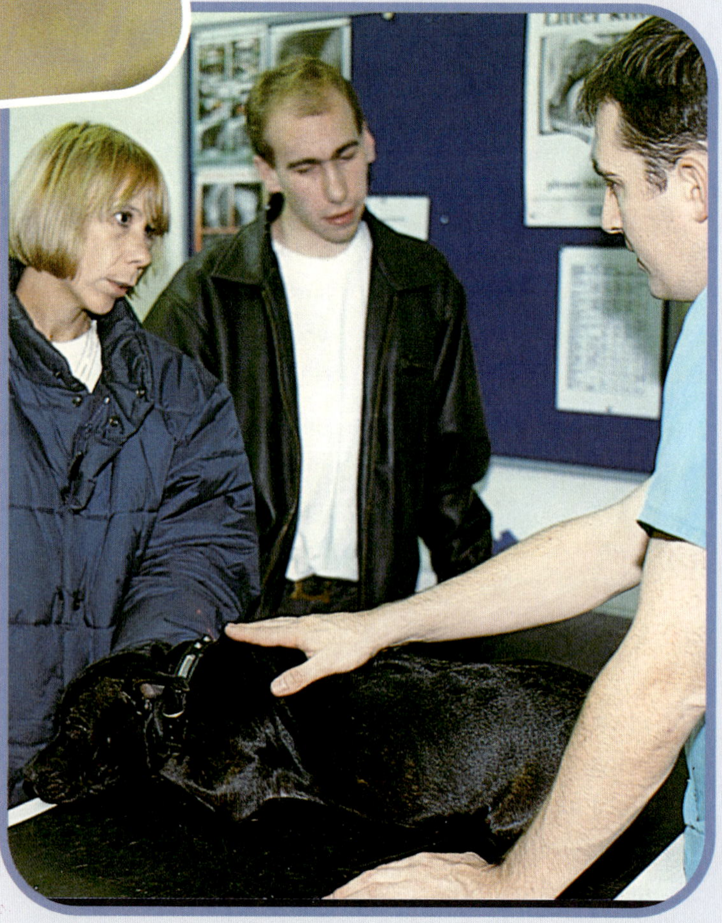

While the vets are busy in their clinics and operating in the theatres, the RSPCA inspectors and animal collection officers are hard at work out and about in London, responding to reports of accidents or sightings of sick wildlife, or investigating allegations of mistreatment and cruelty. When the familiar white van pulls up outside the hospital no one knows what to expect.

Today ACO (Animal Collection Officer) Pauline Beniston has arrived with a large and very frightened patient trussed up in a special green jacket. This beautiful swan has been reported injured. She is heavy, but not dangerous. Pauline says it is a myth that swans are vicious - they only really attack when they are protecting their young. Pauline carries the patient into the prep room where Tessa Bailey is immediately ready to examine her. She has a lot of dried blood on her white feathers. Swans are often accidental casualties – getting caught in fishing tackle or crash landing! Sometimes they even hit overhead cables while flying.

Tessa examines this bird. She seems very docile and weak, which is not a good sign in a wild animal. Tessa takes a good look under the wings and along the back but can see no obvious injuries. She gives the swan fluids, and since there are no obvious injuries she will be sent to the Swan Sanctuary at Egham where hundreds of sick and injured swans are cared for and safely returned to the wild.

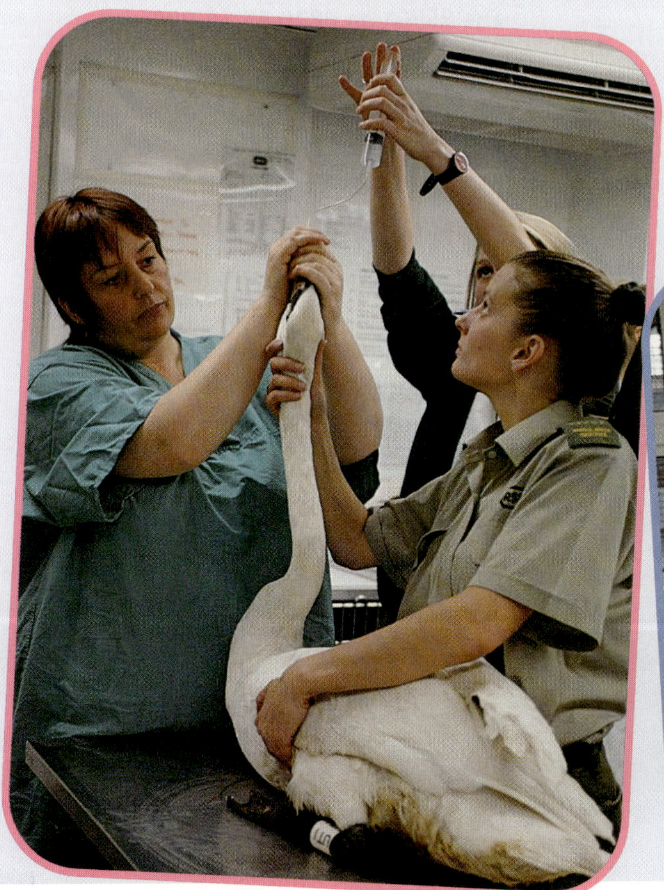

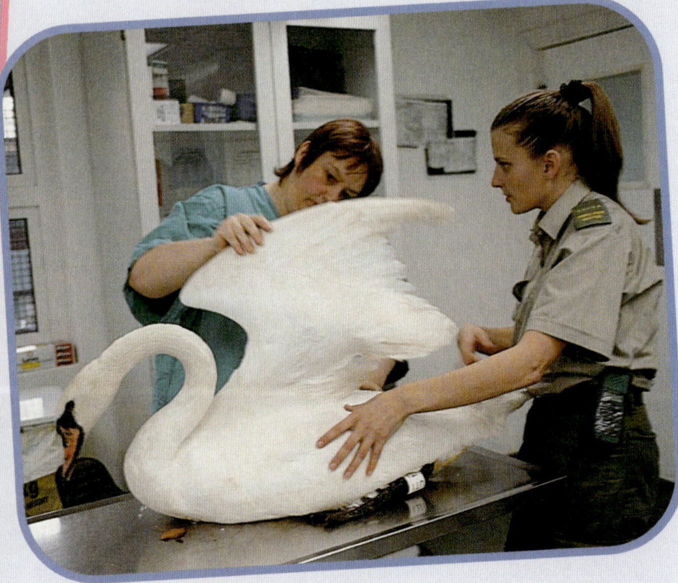

Help!

The animal-friendly problem page.

MY FAMILY IS PLANNING NEXT YEAR'S HOLIDAY. LAST YEAR WHEN WE LEFT OUR DOG IN KENNELS, I REALLY MISSED HER. COULD WE TAKE HER WITH US NEXT TIME?

Yes – if you go on holiday in Great Britain. Ask at your local bookshop or newsagent for a book called Pet's Welcome which lists holiday accommodation that accepts animal, as well as human, guests! Although you could take your cat or dog to some places abroad, it's best not to.

I'VE NOTICED A STRAY DOG RUNNING AROUND IN THE PARK. WHAT SHOULD I DO?

Your local authority employs special dog wardens to collect stray dogs. Contact them or your local police station.

MY DOG HAS BEEN MISSING FOR TWO DAYS AND NIGHTS. HE ISN'T MICROCHIPPED BUT HE WAS WEARING A COLLAR. WHAT CAN I DO?

Contact your local police station or local council who can put you in touch with the dog warden in your area. You could put up posters in your local newsagent, post office, supermarket and at school, and drop a leaflet through letter boxes in neighbouring streets. Ask your postman and milkman to keep a lookout. Ask your local vets as well!

There are several people you can contact in case someone has found your dog:

The RSPCA on 0870 55 55 999

Pet Search on 01225 705175

Cats Protection on 01403 221927

National Canine Defence League on 020 7837 0006

Pet Match on 0870 1600 999

We hope your dog returns home safely. When he does, make sure you take him to be microchipped.

I HAVE TWO MALE RABBITS AND MY VET HAS SUGGESTED I HAVE THEM CASTRATED. MY FRIEND SAYS IT'S DANGEROUS FOR SMALL ANIMALS TO BE PUT UNDER ANAESTHETIC. IS THIS TRUE?

All operations hold some risk. But with modern techniques the advantages of having your rabbits castrated far outweighs the risks. Male rabbits are not ideal partners but will be happier and may even live longer if the operation is carried out.

WHAT'S THE BEST THING TO DO IF YOU SEE AN ANIMAL KNOCKED DOWN BY A CAR?

In any emergency you must try to keep calm. Approach the animal carefully. If it is unconscious or bleeding call a vet immediately. Try to give as many details as possible. Return to the animal and talk softly and use a coat or blanket to keep it warm while you wait.

MY HAMSTER HAS DIED AND I FEEL VERY SAD. DO YOU THINK I SHOULD GET ANOTHER ONE TO REPLACE IT?

It is quite normal to feel very upset when a pet dies. You must allow yourself time to come to terms with its loss. It's a good idea to hold a special ceremony to say goodbye. Remind yourself that you have given your pet a happy life. If you feel the time is right to get a new one, that's fine. Your old pet still holds a special place in your heart.

I'M WORRIED THAT MY DOG HAS WORMS. WHAT SHOULD I DO?

It is very common for cats and dogs to have worms. Often they are hard to detect. Some kinds of worms are a risk to humans so it is important that your dog is treated. Your vet will prescribe the right kind of treatment. It is important to take your dog to the vet regularly to check for signs of worms.

Special Report - from the RSPCA's Stapeley Grange Wildlife Hospital and Cattery

Stapeley Grange is a house with a long history! For many generations it belonged to the Weaver family until it became home to the last surviving family member, Cynthia. When she married her name became Cynthia Zur Nedden, but she never had any children. When her husband died she was left alone with the two passions in her life - her home and her animals. She would spend many hours sitting in her favourite drawing room watching the wildlife in the garden - birds and squirrels by day, foxes and badgers by night. On her death, in 1990 at the age of 82, she bequeathed the Grange and all its land to the RSPCA so that her home could be devoted to the care of animals.

It took four years to transform the house into the RSPCA wildlife hospital that stands today.

Cynthia's drawing room is now the magnificent Discovery Room created by wildlife artist Roger Oakes. Here groups of children, under the expert eye of school liaison officer Neil Barnett, learn about ways they can help preserve and protect our countryside and wildlife. Cynthia's garden has become a haven for wildlife with pond and meadow areas, feeders and plants to attract birds and insects.

Beyond the garden are pools where swans and ducks swim in secure surroundings and purpose-built aviaries where birds of prey perch and fly, while they await careful release back into the wild.

Inside, the house has been transformed into a "fully equipped" wildlife hospital with an operating theatre and X-ray room, laboratory and intensive care unit, isolation wards and oiled-bird cleaning facilities.

The hospital is run by a team of trained staff and skilled volunteers whose aim is to treat and care for patients so that they can be returned, safe and well, to their natural habitat.

The patients arrive here at any time of day and night and come in all shapes and sizes!
Badgers hit by cars, bats caught by cats, foxes trapped in snares, swans harmed by fishermen's hooks and orphans of all kinds. When they arrive at Stapeley Grange the care they receive is their only chance of survival.

TAKE A LOOK INSIDE AND SEE WHICH ANIMALS ARE BEING TREATED HERE TODAY.

IN THE OPERATING THEATRE...

Wildlife vet Ghislaine Sayers is treating an old fox found running around in circles on a housing estate. At first she thought it might have been in a road traffic accident, but as there are no signs of injury, she suspects a middle-ear infection has affected the fox's balance. She treats him with antibiotics to fight the infection.

Suddenly a driver rushes in with a moorhen that has been hit and stunned by his car. Ghislaine can see that the bird is very shocked. She explains that one of the major problems when dealing with wild animals is that they are very stressed by being handled. She must act quickly. The sooner the bird can be put somewhere warm and quiet, the greater its chance of recovery. She checks that there are no breaks in its legs or wings and gives it fluids and painkillers. She also weighs the patient so that she can check on whether it is eating when it starts to recover.

IN THE FLEDGLING ROOM...

At this time of year the room is quiet. But in springtime it will be full of tiny orphaned chicks and cubs who need constant attention if they are to survive. The RSPCA has a strict policy never to return an animal to the wild unless it has made a complete recovery and is strong enough to fend for itself.

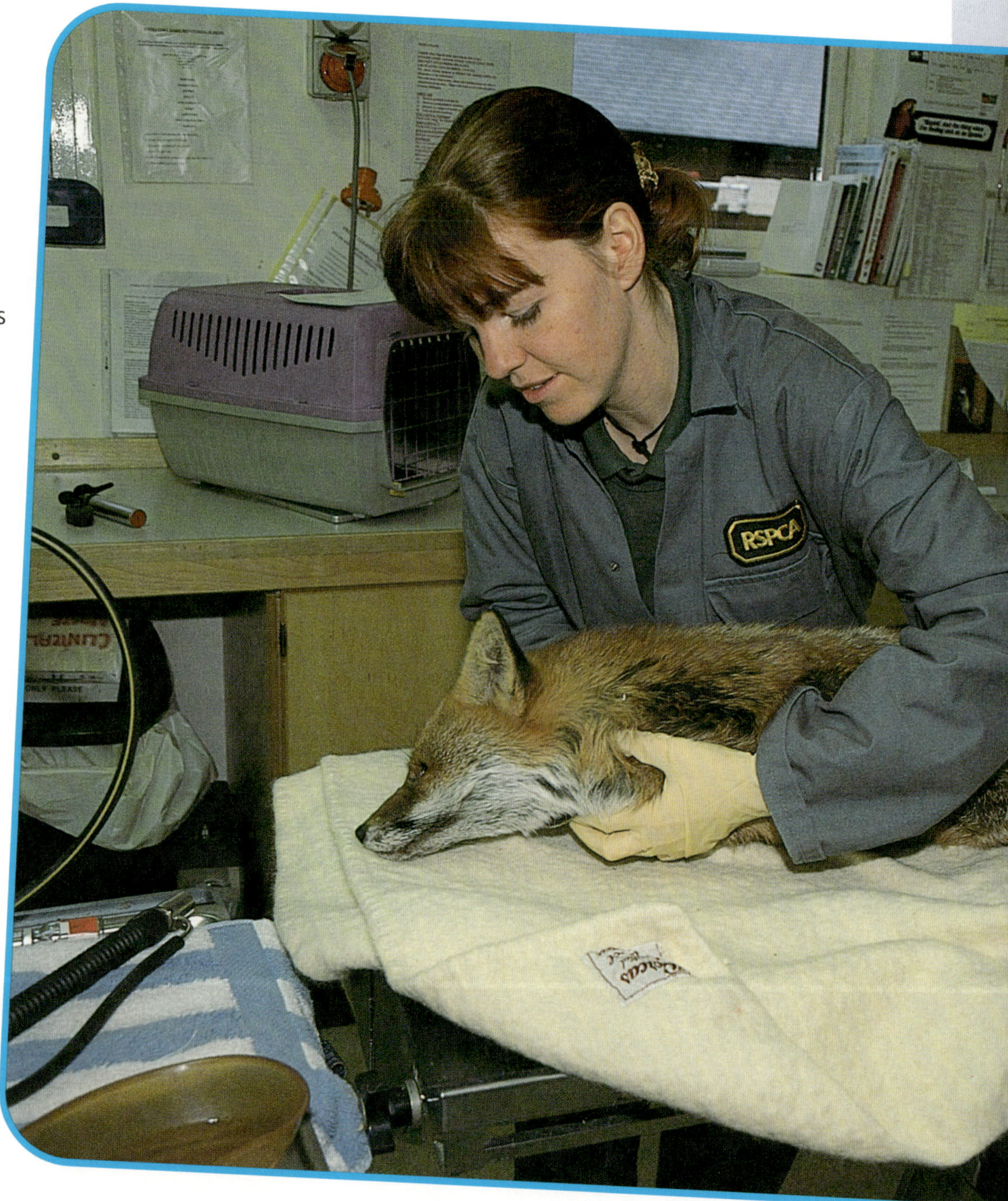

IN THE HOLDING ROOMS...

Meanwhile, fast asleep under layers of shredded paper and special upturned trays, are several sleepy hedgehogs. One was brought in on bonfire night with a firework tied to its middle. The poor little creature was so badly burned that staff didn't expect him to survive. But he did! And now he is recovering well. Another hedgehog is on a special diet of puppy food designed to help him put on weight. Hedgehogs need to weigh over 500 grams before they can hibernate and awake in the spring fully fit and ready for the new season. This patient only weighed 300 grams when he arrived. But now he has almost trebled his body weight so will soon be ready to return to the wild.

IN THE ISOLATION UNIT...

Patients are moved here when they need peace and quiet to help their recovery or when they might be carrying infection.

In the first room is a fox with a badly broken leg. Further along is a cygnet with lead poisoning. Ghislaine explains that even though it is now illegal for fishermen to use lead on their lines, in many waterways there is still so much lying at the bottom of lakes and ponds that it is a constant danger to birds who feed there. And it can be fatal.

This cygnet has had its stomach flushed out twice to remove the lead, but often it can enter the bloodstream and damage the liver or kidneys. Swans hate to be kept inside and are very nervous of humans. Luckily Ghislaine decides that this cygnet is well enough to be allowed out with the others.

ON THE POOLS...

Here are some of the luckier patients who are well on the way to recovery. Staff monitor all the birds very closely. Wildlife assistant James Hogg-Robinson has the tricky task of catching one duck to be weighed. The swans are very protective of the little duck and try to keep James away!

IN THE AVIARY...

Birds of prey, like this beautiful barn owl, can only be returned to the wild if they make a 100% recovery as they depend on their speed and flying ability to survive.

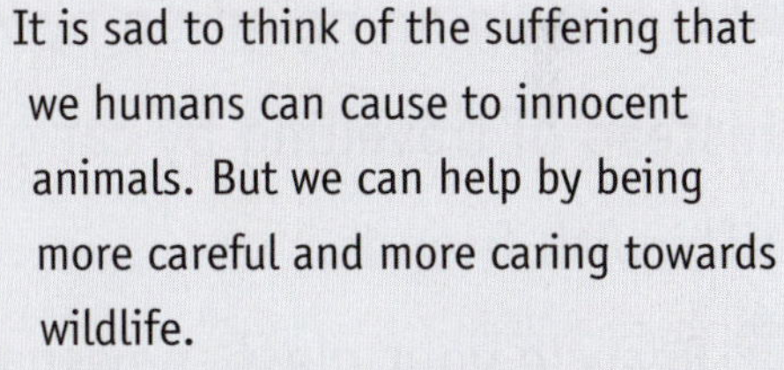

It is sad to think of the suffering that we humans can cause to innocent animals. But we can help by being more careful and more caring towards wildlife.

Some say that Cynthia Zur Nedden was a rather strange old lady. There is even a rumour that she still visits the Grange in a ghostly form! But everyone agrees that she would be delighted with the way things have turned out. Thanks to her generosity wild animals across the North-West can be treated and cared for by the RSPCA.

Time Out for ...NATURE

Our planet is in danger.
Many of our natural resources are in short supply.
Technology is polluting the air we breathe.
Our seas and rivers are being poisoned with toxic waste.
And every year more and more plant and animal species are under threat of extinction.

We all need to improve our appreciation of nature.
We can all take better care of our environment.
Here are some of the ways that YOU can make a difference!

- Cut down on pollution by walking or cycling instead of travelling by car or arrange to share lifts with friends.
- Recycle your glass, newspapers and aluminium cans - recycling saves energy and resources.
- Use recycled products whenever possible - look out especially for products made from recycled paper.
- Support conservation groups in your area.
- Never drop litter.
- Spend a day with your friends finding out more about your local wildlife.
- Plan an animal-friendly garden either at home or at school.

FIND OUT MORE ABOUT THE WILDLIFE IN YOUR BACK GARDEN...

Bury a jam jar or yogurt pot in the soil in your garden so that the top is level with the ground. Put some food into the bottom - a small piece of meat or a drop of jam. Arrange stones around the neck and rest a piece of wood on the top. Leave overnight and you'll be amazed at how many creatures you have collected in the morning. See if you can identify them, and then safely let them go.

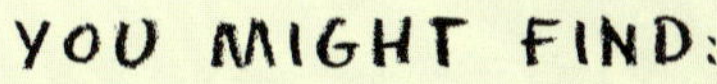

YOU MIGHT FIND:

CENTIPEDE - useful to gardeners as it eats garden pests

MILLIPEDE - has about 100 pairs of legs but only moves slowly

EARWIG - feeds on dead insects, leaves and fruit

SLUG - they have one large 'foot' along the base of their body with their stomach inside it!

WOODLOUSE - if disturbed, it will roll itself into a tight ball. Not actually an insect, but belongs to the same class of animals as crabs and lobsters!

SPIDER - there could be up to one million spiders in an average-sized garden!

Remember: small creatures are just as important as bigger ones.

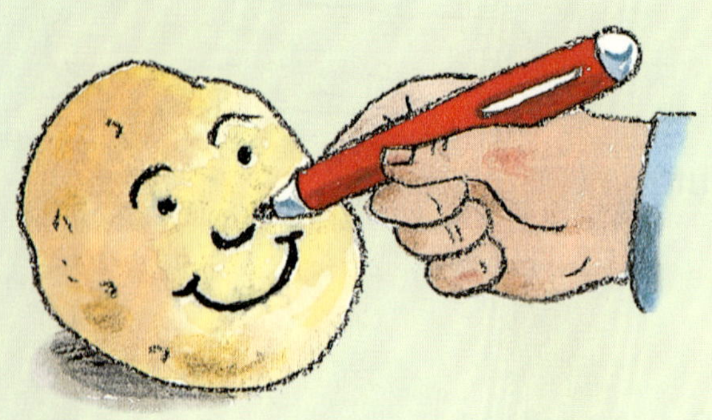

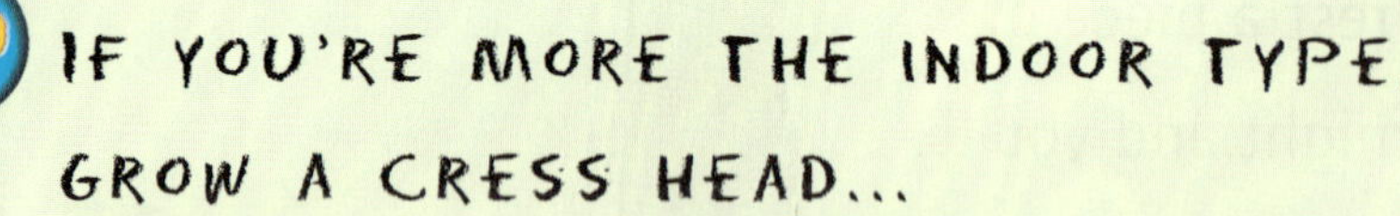

IF YOU'RE MORE THE INDOOR TYPE, GROW A CRESS HEAD...

Draw a face on a large potato and ask a grown-up to make small holes in the top with a cocktail stick. Push cress seeds down into the holes. Make sure the potato stays moist and your 'head' will soon sprout a fine mop of green hair!

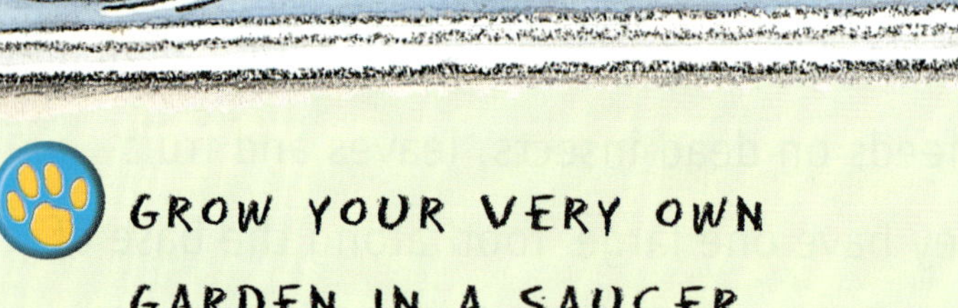

GROW YOUR VERY OWN GARDEN IN A SAUCER...

Here's an easy way to watch the wonders of nature without venturing outside!
Cut the tops from a variety of vegetables – try carrots, beetroot and parsnips.
Stand them in a saucer of water and put them on a well-lit windowsill...

IT'S YOUR PLANET - MAKE IT YOUR BUSINESS TO CARE

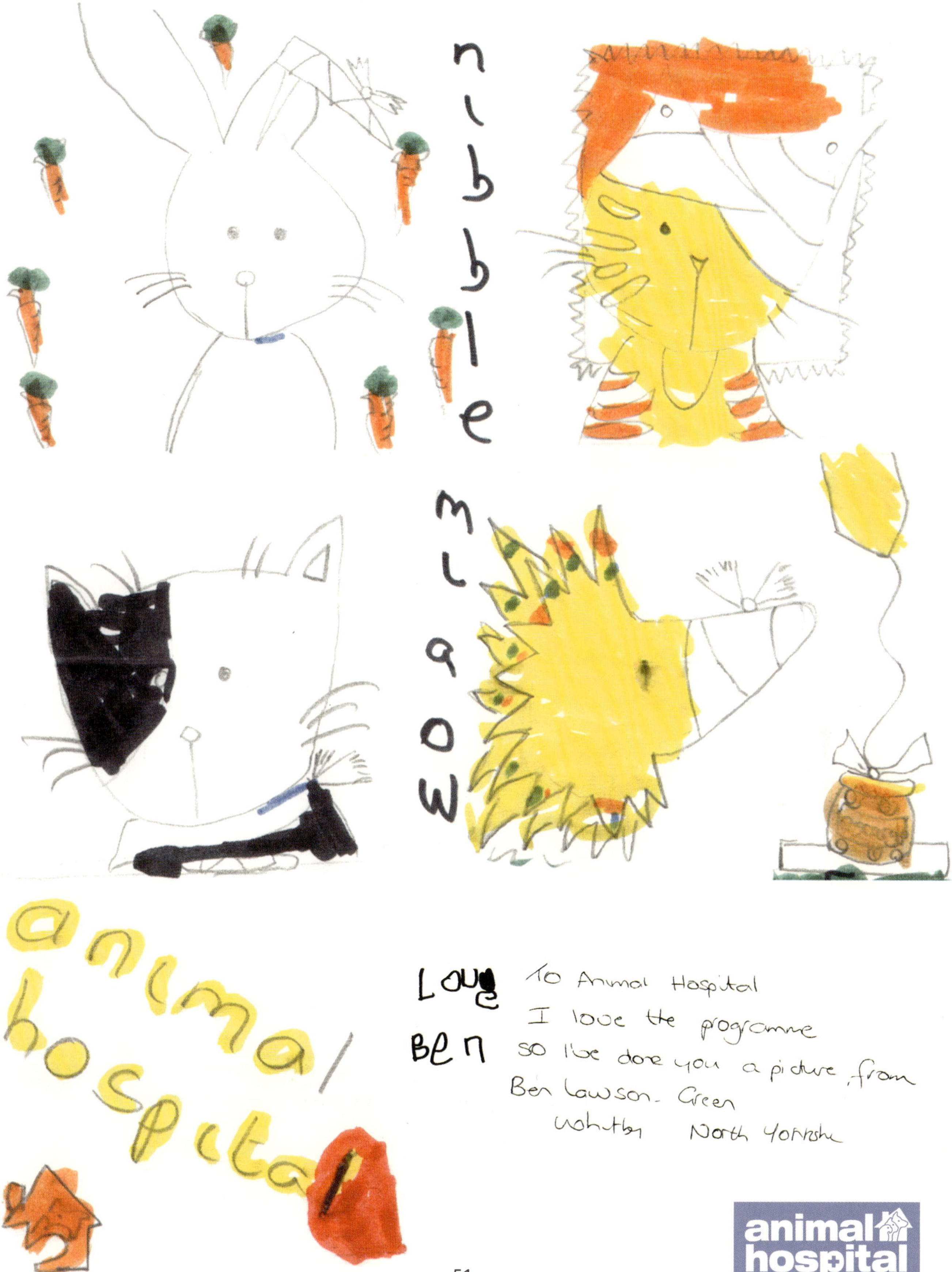

nibble

miaow

Love
Ben

To Animal Hospital
I love the programme
so I've done you a picture, from
Ben Lawson-Green
Whitby North Yorkshire

Home Alone?

You don't have to look far to see an interesting collection of wildlife – in fact, there are probably lots in the room with you right now! Your home is home to all kinds of animals and insects. Houses make good hunting grounds and nesting places – you just have to know where to look!

CHIMNEY
LOFT
ROOF
OUTSIDE
ANIMALS TO SPOT:
CHIMNEY – birds
ROOF – birds' nests
LOFT – grey squirrels
BEDROOM
wardrobe – moths
light – insects
BATHROOM
bath – spiders
LIVING ROOM
behind pictures – spiders
ceiling – spiders
fireside – your cat or dog!
house plants – insects
chair – furniture beetles
floor – carpet beetles
KITCHEN
skirting board – ants
floor – woodlice
cupboards – flies
windowsill – birds
larder – mice
OUTSIDE
doorstep -
slugs and hedgehogs

Time Out for ...JOKES

Where would you find a pink donkey?
Exactly where you left it!

Why did the cat join the RSPCA?
Because he wanted to be a first-aid kit!

What do hedgehogs eat with their cheese?
Prickled onions!

What's as big as a dinosaur but doesn't weigh an ounce?
His shadow!

What has four legs and can fly?
Two birds!

What do you call a horse in a phone box?
Stuck!

Rabbits can multiply - but only a snake can be **an adder!**

What do you call ducks that swim in milk?
Cream quackers!

Why did the fish go on a diet?
He was too heavy for his scales!

How do you stop moles digging in your garden?
Hide the spades!

Which dog wears glasses?
A cock-eyed spaniel!

Why couldn't the butterfly go to the dance?
It was a moth ball!

COMPETITION: 1 

50 super Animal Hospital prizes to be won courtesy of Gosh International plc

Here's an easy-to-enter competition all you have to do is answer this simple question:

How many legs does a spider have?

Write your answer on a postcard or the back of a sealed envelope
(don't forget to put your name, address and age) and post to:

'Animal Hospital Annual Competition'
Egmont World Ltd, Deanway Technology Centre, Wilmslow Road, Handforth, Cheshire SK9 3FB
(Closing date for entries is 26th January 2001)

First Prize
Inflatable Ambulance 6' Play Tent (with pump)

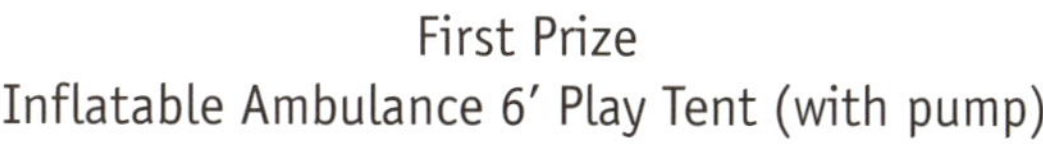

Second Prize
Inflatable Hospital 4' Play Tent (with pump)

Plus 48 super runners-up prizes of:
neck pens, large pencil cases, school sets
and ring binders

COMPETITION: 2

Because you really love animals, the RSPCA Animal Action Club
has given us 100 Animal Action Club memberships to give away!

Animal Action Club members receive a bumper joining pack, filled with information on animals, plus six issues a year of *Animal Action* – the fab young people's magazine, crammed with animal news, celebrity interviews, creature features, competitions, puzzles and games.

How to Enter

To be in with a chance of winning a free membership, simply tell us the name of the very famous presenter of BBC's *Animal Hospital* and, in not more than 20 words, tell us why *Animal Hospital* is your favourite television programme.

Write your entry for this competition on a postcard or the back of a sealed envelope
(don't forget to tell us your name, address and date of birth!) and send it to:

Animal Action Club/Animal Hospital Annual Competition,
Egmont World Ltd, Deanway Technology Centre, Wilmslow Road,
Handforth, Cheshire, SK9 3FB.
Closing date for entries is 26th January 2001!

GOOD LUCK!

Rules:
1 150 winners will be chosen at random and notified by post.
2 Judges' decision will be final. No correspondence will be entered into.
3 The winners' names will be made available from Egmont World Ltd and the RSPCA on request, after 5th February 2001. Please enclose a stamped, self-addressed envelope.
4 Employees (and their relatives) of Egmont World Ltd, the RSPCA and their associated companies are not eligible to enter.
5 Entries are limited to one per person
6 Competition is open to residents of the UK, Channel Islands and Ireland only.
7 The Publishers reserve the right to vary prizes, subject to availability.
8 Closing date for entries is 26th January 2001.

The RSPCA staff at Putney Animal Hospital have some important messages for all **Animal Hospital** fans:

"Exotic animals should NOT be kept as pets. We see all kinds of exotic creatures at Putney. People don't realise how expensive and difficult it is to keep them. A while ago everyone wanted to keep turtles as pets because of the Ninja Turtles craze. But they aren't a toy! Now there are ponds all over London where people have dumped their unwanted turtles and in turn these have killed off all the native wildlife. The creatures belong in tropical countries. I'd ask all the readers never to even consider keeping tropical animals as pets."

ADAM TJOLLE, VET

"So much cruelty to animals is caused by people who just don't understand what their pet needs or how to look after it properly. Animals get into a dreadful state not because their owners are cruel, but just through ignorance. Things like diet, vaccinations, worming, controlling fleas, neutering - all these things are so important."

DEBBIE CLARKE, HOSPITAL MANAGER

"Please, please, please have your pet microchipped. There's nothing sadder than having a well-loved cat or dog brought here when you know its owner is probably pining away somewhere, too. Your pet could end up in a cage feeling lost and homeless. Be responsible."

SARAH THOMAS, VET

"Have your male rabbits and guinea pigs castrated. It is better for the animal and for you. Not only do they become less aggressive, they also get fewer infections and live longer! So if you really love your pet, take it to the vet!"

ADAM TJOLLE, VET

A Funny Thing Happened...

Every grown-up has a favourite funny story about something that happened at work. But staff at an RSPCA hospital see stranger things than most!

HERE ARE SOME OF OUR FAVOURITE ANECDOTES:

MARK BUGGIE:

"I rescued a lovely dog from a flat in Woolwich. When I filled out the paperwork I put my initials on the top, followed by the number of animals rescued:

M-A-B-1. When the dog was chosen to appear on a children's BBC programme they thought my initials were her name – and so she became MABEL from Blue Peter!"

TESSA BAILEY:

"I've treated a kinkajou and racoon – and a flamingo. The poor bird had lost its foot – which is pretty awkward when you spend a lot of time standing on one leg! We had to make it an artificial foot to stand on!"

MARK BUGGIE

"I've rescued dolphins from the Thames and saved seals from under Tower Bridge."

SARAH THOMAS, VET:

"I once took a pair of woolly tights out of an Old English sheepdog!"

ADAM TJOLLE:

"Nothing surprises me any more! I might be treating a dog or cat one minute and a stray iguana or 3.6 metre python the next!"

S...S...S...SPIDERS... Up Close

• Most spiders are harmless to humans, but some can be dangerous – it's advisable to avoid black widows and tarantulas!

• The largest spider is the aptly named Goliath bird-eating spider, which is the size of a dinner plate!

• Spiders are NOT insects (with six legs) but arachnids (with eight legs).

• Spiders kill their prey by stabbing them with their fangs and injecting them with venom.

• Most spiders have eight eyes – but some of them still can't see very well!

• Spiders digest their prey outside the body then suck up the fluid like a kind of soup – YUK!

• A spider's web is made of silk which is as stretchy as elastic and stronger than steel!

• Female spiders are normally bigger than males.

• Most spiders will happily eat other spiders!

Creepy Puzzles

Colour in the dotted areas of this web to see what this spider has caught!

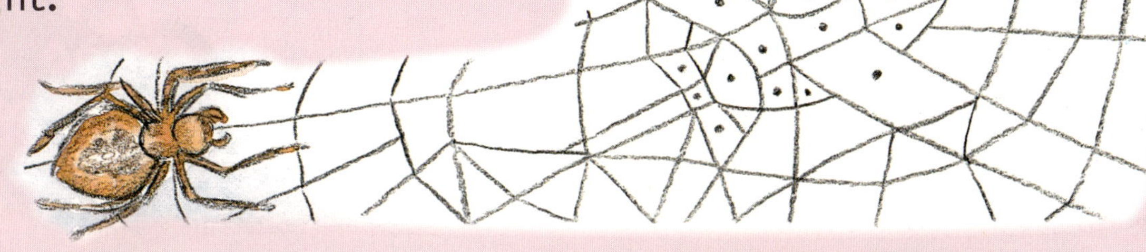

There are ten differences between these pictures. Can you find them all?

These four spiders each think they have caught something tasty for tea! Can you untangle their threads to see which one is right?

Time Out for a Quiz

 True or false? 

You've read this annual from cover to cover and learned lots of interesting facts! But how many can you remember? To find out, answer 'true' or 'false' to these questions...

1. A hamster can have up to 18 babies at once.

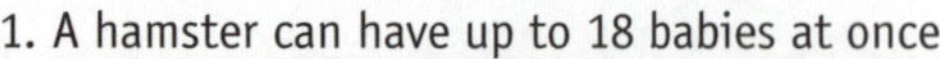

6. A spider is an insect.

2. There are 240 recognised breeds of dog.

7. You have to be 22 to become an RSPCA Inspector.

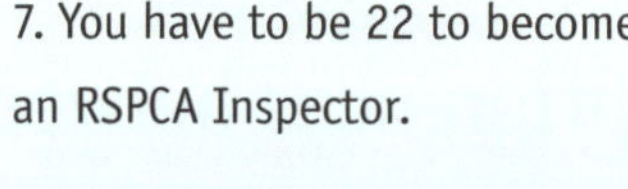

3. Queen Victoria put the 'Royal' into the RSPCA.

8. Hamsters live on average for 5 years.

4. Foxes like to hibernate in winter.

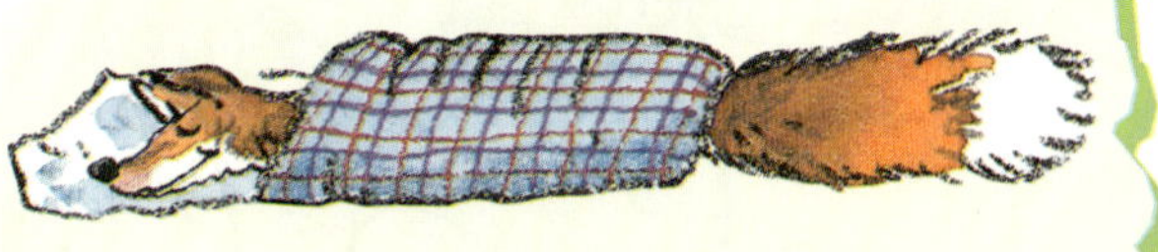

9. You should contact your local police station or dog warden if you see a stray dog.

5. It takes 5 years to train as a vet.

10. Most spiders have 8 eyes.

HOW DID YOU DO?
TRY THESE QUESTIONS OUT ON A GROWN-UP AND SEE IF THEY CAN DO BETTER!

All the Answers and Addresses

The Official Rolf Harris Fan Club:
PO Box 396, Northampton, NN5 6ZW

RSPCA: Causeway, Horsham, West Sussex RH12 1HG

RSPCA website: www.rspca.org.uk

ANSWERS:

PAGE 13

1. **dog**-eared ... battered and worn
dogfish ... a small shark
doghouse ... where you go when you've been bad
dogleg ... sharp corner on a race track
dogmatic ... opinionated and arrogant
dogma ... religious code of beliefs
dog paddle ... first swimming stroke
dogsbody ... person who does all the chores
dogged ... very determined

2. LASSIE, SCOOBY DOO, PLUTO, BEETHOVEN, MUTTLEY, GNASHER

3.

C	H	L	A	B	R	A	D	O	R
O	P	O	O	D	L	E	S	G	D
R	C	O	L	L	I	E	H	R	A
G	H	J	M	N	S	S	E	E	L
I	V	B	K	L	X	T	E	Y	M
X	S	D	F	G	E	E	P	H	A
H	U	S	K	Y	I	G	D	O	T
T	U	E	G	V	F	F	O	U	I
S	P	A	N	I	E	L	G	N	O
A	L	S	A	T	I	A	N	D	N

PAGE 29

1. **ham** burger
ham mer
ham mock
ham per
ham sandwich

2.

A	Y	D	F	D	A	E	R	K
A	D	R	G	H	J	F	H	L
G	H	N	M	K	H	J	H	G
D	F	G	U	R	R	D	F	G
B	V	B	K	T	A	L	J	H
B	A	A	R	Y	S	A	D	A
A	M	E	G	V	F	K	A	V
D	J	K	B	E	K	V	F	V
F	G	Y	H	D	M	F	K	H

PAGE 59

The green spider.

ROLF HARRIS YOU ARE THE BEST.
ANIMAL HOSPITAL BBC
ANIMAL
HOSPITA
IS THE
BEST